Endors

"I am overjoyed to see Cotton Mather's *Christianity to the Life* again in print! While some older works struggle to find relevance with a modern audience, this little gem is as timely and fresh as ever. Garnetta Smith has blessed us by doing the heavy lifting, offering a new edition with helpful explanatory notes. Additionally, Joseph Harrod and Michael Haykin provide insightful introductory material that will place the reader in the world and mind of our beloved brother Cotton. May the brilliance and vibrancy of Christ ever shine forth in these pages."

—**Nate Pickowicz**, Pastor, Harvest Bible Church, Gilmanton Iron Works, NH; author, *Reviving New England*; editor, The American Puritan series

"Many treasured reflections of the Christian church are out of print or not otherwise easily accessible. Prior to this expertly edited and helpfully notated copy of *Christianity to the Life*, by Cotton Mather (1663–1728), I would not have even known about this nourishing biblical sermon. Mrs. Garnetta Smith has done us all a great service in publishing this spiritual feast of practical Christian instruction."

—**Robert L. Plummer**, Ph.D., Chairman, New Testament Department; Professor of New Testament Interpretation, The Southern Baptist Theological Seminary

"*Christianity to the Life*, by Cotton Mather (1663–1728), presents Christians with a timely imperative to imitate Christ as they walk like him in all holiness. Based on Christ's work for us at Calvary, Mather is explicit about the Bible's call to obedience. This short book is powerfully written and well organised, and Garnetta's excellent editorial skills have made it extremely accessible and practical for Christians today. Read it devotionally or simply for edification. Either way you'll be blessed."

—**Gavin Peacock**, Associate Pastor, Calvary Grace Church of Calgary; Director of International Outreach for CBMW; co-author of *The Grand Design: Male and Female He Made Them* (Christian Focus)

"Read *Christianity to the Life* in one sitting as the Sunday morning sermon it was intended. Then take the book and read it devotionally savoring each morsel. Your Spirit will be nourished by the solid food of the exposited Word of God. The church is indebted to Mrs. Garnetta Smith for her modernization and republication of Cotton Mather's timeless exhortation to walk in holiness by imitating our Lord and Savior, Jesus Christ."

—**Terry Delaney**, Pastor, Union Baptist Church, Mexico, Missouri; Book Review Editor, ChristianBookNotes.com

CHRISTIANITY TO THE LIFE:
A CALL TO IMITATE CHRIST

COTTON MATHER

Edited by GARNETTA SWEENEY SMITH

Christianity TO THE LIFE

A Call to Imitate Christ

Foreword by JOSEPH C. HARROD
Introduced by MICHAEL A.G. HAYKIN

H&E
Publishing

CONTENTS

Acknowledgments

It would have been impossible for me to complete a project such as this without significant expert assistance from my colleagues at The Southern Baptist Theological Seminary.

This project began originally as an assignment in a church history course. My professor, Dr. Joseph Harrod, suggested that I seek to have my transcription of Cotton Mather's sermon published. Thank you, Dr. Harrod, for the idea, introduction to the publisher, your constant encouragement, and for writing the foreword to what is now my first published book.

Dr. Michael Haykin, I could never adequately thank you for writing such a wonderful introduction to this publication. I would still be reading and studying about Cotton Mather to have a few feeble words to introduce this wonderful sermon and its author had you not so generously given of your time, expertise, and wealth of knowledge.

I am humbled by the generosity of Dr. Rob Plummer and Dr. Tyler Flatt who translated and provided commentary for the Greek and Latin phrases, respectively, from Mather's sermon. Thank you.

Mrs. Marsha Omanson, thank you for encouraging my educational pursuits for the past ten years. I am a grateful recipient of your wisdom and knowledge, but most importantly, your friendship.

Editor's Note

In this edition, the punctuation and capitalization have been modernized, some archaic words have been updated, and a few other slight editorial changes made. Where archaic or obsolete words have been retained they are defined in footnotes. The text was not completely modernized, especially Scripture references, as I wanted to maintain the mood and weightiness of the language of the era. All definitions are from the Oxford English Dictionary unless otherwise noted.

About the Editor

Garnetta is the Women's Support Coordinator and Director of the Center for Student Success at The Southern Baptist Theological Seminary in Louisville, Kentucky. Along with a Master of Arts in Biblical Counseling, she possesses a Master of Theology, and is a candidate for the Doctor of Education (2020). She and her husband Lawrence recently celebrated their 40th wedding anniversary. Their sons Jason and Edward, along with his wife, Rachael, live nearby.

Dedication

To my parents, Mr. and Mrs. Garnett Ellis (Bertha Wilkinson) Sweeney, who always encouraged me to take advantage of educational opportunities they were not afforded.

FOREWORD

Joseph C. Harrod

I am very thankful that this present edition of *Christianity to the Life* has found its way into your hands. This little sermon, long out of print, offers a timeless call for believers to imitate Christ. Imitation is a perennial Christian theme, rooted in Scripture (cf. 1 Corinthians 4:16, 11:1; Ephesians 5:1; Philippians 3:17; 1 Thessalonians 2:14; 2 Thessalonians 3:7; and 3 John 11) and expounded by interpreters such as Origen, Athanasius, Thomas à Kempis, and John Calvin. And here again, in the hands of one of New England's ablest preachers, this theme receives a hearty evangelical treatment, along with careful pastoral application.

I first discovered this sermon years ago from an endnote in Richard Lovelace's *The American Pietism of Cotton Mather*. Apart from Lovelace and perhaps a handful of specialists, I doubt that this sermon had many readers since its initial publication in the early 18th century. Unlike other classics, this work has not been printed and reprinted, translated and shared, discussed and interpreted, but has rather laid silent for many generations.

After my own "discovery" of this work, I began to assign it as required reading for a course on Christian devotional classics both at the Master's and Doctoral levels. It was through this process that the editor of the present edition, Garnetta Sweeney Smith, first discovered the sermon and saw its unique applicability for modern discipleship. I was eager for her to produce a modernized, annotated edition for a class assignment, but am now even more eager for her diligent work to find its way into a wider audience. She has taken care to read Mather closely and to elucidate his sometimes-opaque references with care. I commend her careful and patient work to you and hope that your encounter with Mather and his call to genuine discipleship will be as helpful to you as it was for us.

Louisville, Kentucky
November 2018

PREFACE

Garnetta Sweeney Smith

Transcription of this book began innocuously as an assignment for a seminary course. Three years later, this sermon from 1702 is a new book poised to admonish, challenge, and encourage today's Christian as it surely did over three hundred years ago. Mather, using Romans 2:28, applied to Christians, "... we may say that he is not a Christian that has no more than the name of a Christian. A man must have the walk of a Christian, or else he commits a crime when he pretends the same."[1] Though now three centuries old, I believe this sermon remains quite applicable for 21st century Christians due to its abundance of scriptural references. Though the original document had nearly 90 Scripture references, which were noted parenthetically in the text and remain so, as I read and worked with the text, I discovered 65 additional Scriptures which have been referenced in footnotes to distinguish them from the original work.

This book is a discipleship manual of sorts, providing both the "means of pursuing an imitation of Christ"

---

[1] See below, page 1.

and "the points by which a Christian pursues an imitation of Christ." It is clear that Mather understood the
need to walk worthy of the Lord Jesus Christ and be conformed to Him. His cadence and rhythm in preaching is
often palpable as he pleads with his congregants to follow Christ's example. We would do well to have the
same ambition.

Though the book is short enough to be read quickly,
my prayer is that it will be used as a devotional, with a
Bible close by, to teach Christians what it means and
looks like to imitate Christ, to the glory of God.

INTRODUCTION

Michael A.G. Haykin

Cotton Mather (1663–1728), the scion of a notable Puritan house and the pastor of Boston's Old North Congregational Church, was a prolific author. His writings reveal a thorough acquaintance with more than three hundred authors as they emphasize key evangelical themes like conversion as the unmerited work of the Holy Spirit, personal and social holiness, corporate prayer for revival, the unity of the church and its advance throughout the world, and the importance of family religion. In our day, when social holiness has become a contested matter among Evangelicals, it bears remembering that an early Evangelical like Mather spent considerable energy in founding and supporting a charity school for poor children and orphans as well as a school for educating African American children. The latter Mather paid for out of his own pocket for quite a number of years. The Boston pastor also organized the members of his church into small groups so that all of the spiritual and physical needs of those in the Old North parish—churched and unchurched alike—could be taken care of. Mather was not a wealthy pastor, but, in addition to the charitable works noted above, he frequently used his limited resources to help the needy.[1]

In the sermon below, Mather's concern for personal and social holiness is quite evident in his insistence that a "Christian must be a Christ-like man,"[2] for it is "in the imitation of Christ that we arrive unto holiness."[3] So Mather urges his hearers/readers to let their "hearts bleed with compassion" for their fellow human beings even as Christ acted with compassion towards those bound in misery who came across his path.[4] Mather is emphatic that this pertains not only to spiritual matters but also temporal miseries:

> Be troubled in and for the various troubles which other men are broken withal. Visit the sick and comfort the sad and relieve the needy. Help them in all their wants, by all the ways you can. Devise liberal things; contrive obliging things when you can do nothing else. ... look out for occasions to do good unto all ...[5]

---

[1]Richard F. Lovelace, *Dynamics of Spiritual Life: An Evangelical Theology of Renewal* (Downers Grove, IL: Inter-Varsity Press, 1979), 363–364. Lovelace's biography of Mather is still the best introduction to this Puritan thinker. See his *The American Pietism of Cotton Mather: Origins of American Evangelicalism* (1979 ed.; repr. Eugene, OR: Wipf and Stock, 2007).

[2] See below, page 3.

[3] See below, page 16.

[4] See below, page 47.

[5] See below, page 48.

Imitating Christ is an unexpected theme to find in a classic Evangelical sermon like this one by Mather. We tend to think that this is a Roman Catholic emphasis. But the passionate exegesis with which Mather argues his case is well worth Evangelicals pondering in our day, for here writ large is a deep concern by an early Evangelical voice for both spirituality and social justice. As Mather said in another of his works, *A Christian at his Calling* (1701): "God hath made man a sociable creature. We expect benefits from human society. It is but equal, that human society should receive benefits from us."[6] And those benefits must pertain to both spirit and body.

------

[6]Cotton Mather, *A Christian at his Calling* (Boston, MA: Samuel Sewall, 1701), 37.

1

CHRISTIANITY TO THE LIFE

1 John 2:6
He that saith he abideth in him, ought also himself
so to walk, even as He walked.

My discourse, I suppose, will reach to no person who assumes not unto himself the name of a Christian. Many a person perhaps does, like the blessed Theophilus,[1] rejoice in his wearing this, *Το θεοφιλε'ς ὄνομα,*[2] a name so dear to God. But it greatly becomes and behooves[3] every such person to consider, "What is a Christian?" For if it could be said, "He is not a Jew who is one outwardly" (Romans 2:28), we may say he is not a Christian that has no more than the name of a Christian. A man must have the walk of a Christian, or else he commits a crime when

---

[1] Luke 1:3; Acts 1:1.

[2] "It appears that Mather here is using a mixture of Greek and English—with a possessive English ending on a vocative Greek form." Robert L. Plummer, Professor of New Testament Interpretation, Southern Seminary, Louisville, KY.

[3] *Behooves* meaning to be morally needful or requisite to; to be incumbent, proper, or due.

he pretends the name. It is not everyone that says, "Lord, Lord," unto our Lord Jesus Christ, who is the real Christian; but it is he that walks as the Lord Jesus Christ walked. Of which walk I am now to advise you, O my hearers, with that prayer which a minister once made for his people, "That you may walk worthy of the Lord, unto all well-pleasing; being fruitful in every good work and increasing in the knowledge of God" (Colossians 1:10).

I remember the Apostle Paul directed his Colossians to read the epistle from Laodicea. Now, what was that epistle from Laodicea? It seems to me that it was the First Epistle of John—an epistle that John wrote from Laodicea. Truly, I must now invite you to read the First Epistle of John. We have, and God is exceedingly to be praised that we have in our hands, a brief discourse containing and consisting of but five short chapters, in which the Holy Spirit of God had intimated that all things necessary to everlasting life are contained in it. This is the First Epistle of John and how inexcusable are we if we think much to acquaint ourselves with so small a volume that has in it so great a treasure.

One of the things herein written unto us (that we may have everlasting life) is what has now been read: "He that saith he abideth in Christ ought himself to walk even as Christ walked."[4] There is, in our text supposed, a man pretending to an interest in the Lord Jesus Christ

---

[4] 1 John 2:6.

and a union and fellowship with him. Such a man is here instructed how to justify his pretense; it is to be justified by an imitation of the Lord Jesus Christ.

The great assertion before us is that the imitation of Christ is essential to a Christian.

A man cannot be a Christian without conformity to Christ. A Christian man must be a Christ-like man. Except a man follow the example of the Lord Jesus Christ, it is a vain thing for him to expect blessedness from that holy Lord. The walk of a Christian, or his course of life in this world, must have the walk of the Lord Jesus Christ made the pattern of it. He forfeits the name of a Christian who does not endeavor such a holy walk as what was exemplified in the holy walk of the Lord Jesus Christ.

There are two cases that now lie before us.

2

The Means by Which a Christian Should Pursue an Imitation of Christ

What are the means by which a Christian should pursue an imitation of the Lord Jesus Christ?

In aspiring after that high attainment of Christianity, the imitation of Christ, let a Christian mind these directions.

I. The Holy Walk of Christ as an Example

Let a Christian consider the holy walk of the Lord Jesus Christ, as intended and recorded, for an example to be followed in the walk of every Christian. To preserve right thoughts of this thing is a thing of no little consequence.

Christ Came for More Than Our Example

Now, first, a Christian must not imagine that when our Lord Jesus Christ came among us the sole design, or indeed the chief design, of his coming was to set us an example. God forbid that ever we should fall into the Socinian[1] abomination to dream that the life and the death of our Lord Jesus Christ was only, or chiefly, to set us an example of holy living and dying: an example of exactness in our life and of patience in our death. We are assured, and that man is no Christian who is not assured that "the Son of Man came to give his life a ransom for many."[2]

When the Oracles of God counsel us to follow the example of our Lord Jesus Christ they do observably annex[3] a caution against a vain apprehension, as if he were no more than an example. So, "Walk in love as Christ also hath loved us," (but for our caution is presently follows), "and he hath given himself for us an offering and a sacrifice unto God of a sweet-smelling savour" (Ephesians 5:2). Christians, forget not that the obedience which our Lord Jesus Christ yielded unto God was to be the meritorious and the material cause of our justification as well as the exemplary cause of our sanctification. Yea, we never could have our heart so renewed as to desire and attain the least imitation of our Lord Jesus

---

[1] *Socinian* meaning of or relating to Socinianism or Socinian. Socinianism is a Christian religious movement and doctrine characterized by antitrinitarianism, rationalism, and denial of the divinity of Jesus. Socinianism arose in 16th century Poland as an early form of Unitarianism, being particularly associated with the Italian theologian Laelius Socinus (1525–1562) and his nephew Faustus Socinus (1539–1604). Its tenets were stated in the Racovian Catechism of 1605.

[2] Matthew 20:28; Mark 10:45.

[3] *Annex* meaning to append or add an extra part.

Christ if the obedience of our Lord Jesus Christ unto God had not bought such a heart for us. Our Lord Jesus Christ must be considered by us as not only our Master but also as our "Surety" (Hebrews 7:22). We must not merely imitate our Lord Jesus Christ as giving us an example, but we must likewise trust in him and rest on him as making atonement for us. Indeed, we shall never imitate him till we do so.

It has been a Satanic stratagem[4] to press the imitation of Christ with an intent, thereby, to draw off the minds of men from faith in the satisfaction and propitiation of Christ. That the guiltiness of the first Adam and the righteousness of the second Adam is no otherwise ours than by imitation are two damnable heresies. If they that propound the imitation of the Lord Jesus Christ would not proceed preposterously, let them remember this: Your first work is to apprehend the obedience of the Lord Jesus Christ unto the Law of God, as provided by the grace of God, for your only justifying righteousness. Accept and improve that glorious righteousness of the Lord Jesus Christ as your only title to the eternal happiness of the righteous.

The Most High God, being therefore reconciled unto you, now is the time, here is the place for you to pass on unto as much imitation of what was imitable[5] in

---

[4] *Stratagem* meaning a plan, a scheme; especially one devised to achieve a particular end, gain an advantage, or outwit an opponent—often with the implication of deviousness or dishonesty.

[5] *Imitable* meaning deserving of imitation.

7

the obedience of the Lord Jesus Christ as ever you can. First, get an expiation[6] for the sin of thy soul, Oh man, by relying on that good thing, the Messiah of God. Then, try to do justice and love mercy, and walk humbly, even as he walked.[7] Sirs, you don't receive the righteousness in the obedience of the Lord Jesus Christ provided for you with a due disposition if you be not hereupon disposed unto the imitation of it.

Not All of Christ Is for Our Imitation

Secondly, a Christian must not imagine that everything of the Lord Jesus Christ, the almighty King of heaven, is an example for us—the poor worms of the dust. The sorry children of men may not think to arrive unto the graces and the glories of that Lord who is fairer than the children of men.[8] Our Lord Jesus Christ is that Holy One who may say, "To whom will ye liken me, or shall I be equal?"[9] There were many illustrious types of old wherein God exhibited some resemblances of his Messiah unto the world. But, about the best of them all, we find it said, "Who among the sons of the mighty can be likened unto the Lord?" (Psalm 89:6).

It is possible that the criminal ambition with which Satan inspired our first parents might be after such

---

[6] *Expiation* meaning the action of expiating or making atonement for.
[7] Micah 6:8.
[8] Psalm 45:2.
[9] Isaiah 40:25.

things as were the peculiar prerogatives of the Messiah. There are incommunicable perfections of the Lord Jesus Christ wherein a Christian may not propose to imitate him. As it was said, "Hast thou an arm like God? Or, can you thunder with a voice like him?" (Job 40:9). Even so, can you be personally united unto the second person in God? Or, can you work miracles and command all the armies of heaven as that ever-adorable person can? The supposals[10] were arrogant blasphemies! To talk of being hence Christed[11] with Christ is a nonsensical gibberish to be heard only in the mouth of some delirious Familist.[12] There are also mediatorial performances of the Lord Jesus Christ wherein to imitate him is not proposed unto a Christian. Our Lord Jesus Christ, managing the offices of a Mediator says, "Of the people there is none with me" (Isaiah 63:3).

Indeed, we are in a way of similitude and analogy to do something of what was done by our Lord Jesus Christ as Mediator. The dying and rising of our Lord Jesus Christ is to be imitated in our dying to sin and living to

---

[10] *Supposals* meaning the acts of supposing something, suppositions.

[11] *Christed* meaning made one with Christ, made a partaker of Christ's nature. A word of the 'Familists' in the 17th century.

[12] *Familist* meaning a member of a sect called the "Family of Love" founded by Hendrik Niclaes in the Netherlands during the 1540s. Active in England in the 16th and 17th centuries, the Christian sect held that religion consists chiefly in the exercise of love.

God. There is a charitative[13] intercession wherein we are to mention those of whom our great High Priest is an Intercessor, makes mention at the right hand of God.[14] But, no saint can purchase for, or apply to the elect of God, the blessings of his covenant, nor intercede in his own name for any of those blessings. None but a popish[15] idolater can presume a thing so extravagant. More than all this, I judge there is no need of adding that, in those very matters wherein our Lord Jesus Christ is imitable, we must not account the measures to be attainable. In our Lord Jesus Christ, there is a fullness of those things whereof the best of us can have but a little. In that sanctity wherein we should imitate our Lord Jesus Christ, he must be allowed a preeminence as first-born among many brethren.[16] It must be allowed unto our Lord, "God, thy God, has anointed thee with the oil of gladness above thy fellows" (Psalm 45:7). But then,

Christ's Holiness as our Object for Imitation
Thirdly, a Christian must consider the holiness that was conspicuous in the walk of the most holy Lord Jesus Christ as being set before us, by him, for the perpetual object of our imitation. We cannot walk on the sea[17] or

---

[13] *Charitative* meaning of the nature of, or pertaining to, charity.
[14] Romans 8:34.
[15] *Popish* meaning of or relating to Roman Catholicism or the Roman Catholic Church. Chiefly derogatory.
[16] Romans 8:29.
[17] Matthew 14:26.

walk in the midst of the golden candlesticks[18] like our Lord Jesus Christ. Yet, we are to walk as he walked. How? By imitating the holiness of his conversation which was displayed when he walked more than thirty years in his humiliation[19] among us. Hence, we are called upon, "As he which hath called you is holy, so be you holy in all manner of conversation" (1 Peter 1:14).

Perhaps it is a note more argute[20] than solid that some have had upon that passage, "He opened his mouth and taught them" (Matthew 5:2). What need of such a pleonasm[21] as that "he opened his mouth"? Could he have taught them otherwise? Yes, truly our Lord was frequently teaching the world without opening his mouth unto them. He taught men by walking before them. He taught us what we are to do by his own doing always the things that please the Father.[22]

God's Glory Is the True State of the Case
The true state of the case is this: The Almighty God has given his commandments to us as the everlasting and unrepealable and unalterable rule in our observation by

---

[18] Revelation 2:1.

[19] *Humiliation* referring to Christ's coming to earth as a man.

[20] *Argute* meaning to be quick, sharp, keen, subtle, especially in small matters.

[21] *Pleonasm* meaning the use of more words in a sentence or clause than are necessary to express the meaning; redundancy of expression either as a fault of style, or as a rhetorical figure used for emphasis or clarity.

[22] John 8:29.

which he will be glorified. For to speak as if God had abrogated[23] and abolished or abated that eternal rule of our glorifying him is indeed the truest antinomianism.[24] Now, we poor weak ignorant creatures know not after what manner or by what sort of walk that rule is to be observed wherefore the Son of God, becoming a man, he was put under the Law. He, having made satisfaction for our sins against the Law, the God of heaven, then gives this admonition unto us, "Behold a living law. Look unto my holy Jesus and from his keeping of the Law, do you, O Sons of Men, learn how to live unto the glory of him that has redeemed you, pardoned you, adopted you."

There are four inspired historians[25] that have left unto us a narrative of our Lord's walk upon the earth for several years together. The gospel has, like the chariot of our Lord-Redeemer, been drawn by those four historians as by four cherubim unto all the four quarters of the earth. The walk of our Lord is in these invaluable memorials reported unto us. We see a greater than Solomon[26] described unto us in the reports of the sacred pages. At the bottom of all, we may for a motto conceive those words as coming from the mouth of our Lord: "What ye

---

[23] *Abrogated* meaning repealed (a law, established usage, etc.); abolished authoritatively or formally.

[24] *Antinomianism* meaning the doctrine or practice of antinomians; avowed rejection of the moral law.

[25] The four gospel writers.

[26] Matthew 12:42.

have seen me do, make haste, and do as I have done" (Judges 9:48).

Christ's Command to Walk as He Walked
Our Lord Jesus Christ hath now expressly told us that in his holy Walk he purposed an example for us. This was the voice of our Lord Jesus Christ: "I have given you an example that ye should do as I have done" (John 13:15). Thus, we read, "Christ hath left us an example, that we should follow his steps" (1 Peter 2:21). It is what our Lord has enjoined upon us all: "If any man serve me, let him follow me" (John 12:26). Hence, there is an exhortation that speaks unto us in those terms, "Put on the Lord Jesus Christ" (Romans 13:14), which is as much as to say, "Let your walk be such, as to show much of the Lord Jesus Christ in it, that they who see you may see much of the Lord Jesus Christ upon you."

Likewise, we read, "As ye have received Christ Jesus the Lord, so walk in him" (Colossians 2:6), which is to say, "Walk even as he walked." [27]

II. The Obligation to Imitate Christ's Example
Let a Christian consider the vast obligation that lies upon him to walk with an imitation of the example which the Lord Jesus Christ, in his holy walk, has given him. That we may walk as the Lord Jesus Christ walked, we must be stirred up to such a walk. A man won't walk till

---

[27] 1 John 2:6.

13

he is awake. Now, Christian, stir up yourself with such thoughts as these.

Christ's Walk Is the Walk of a Christian
First, a Christian should think, "What is all my religion, but a vain opinion, if I have not the religious walk of a Christian?" It is the imitation of Christ that is the walk of a Christian. Many a man will make a profession of religion and it may be the man's profession will be signalized by a zeal for some singular opinion in the Christian religion. But know it, sirs, Christianity lies not in talking, but in walking.

We read of a sect "that would pay with tithes and omit the weightier matters of the Law" (Matthew 23:23). There are some of a sectarian spirit that will be zealous for the particular and peculiar opinion of their own parties in Christianity, but they omit the weightier matters in Christianity. It will be no matter with them whether they be in the fear of the Lord all the day long and whether they wash their hearts from all wicked lusts and whether they keep their tongues from evil, or, whether they walk as the Lord Jesus Christ walked, or no. By this device of Satan it is that Christianity is almost ruined in the world. Men are not concerned about the vitality of Christianity, but only about some notions in it.

Men are not Christians because the chief of their Christianity lies not in the imitation of Christ, but in being such or such a sort of Christian. My neighbors, this Christianity will nothing avail you. If all a man's religion lie in an opinion he has but an opinion of a religion. That is to say, as the apostle speaks, he only seems to be religious and his religion is vain. Christianity turns upon higher points than mere niceties of opinion: "Not meat and drink, but righteousness, and peace and joy in the Holy Ghost" (Romans 14:17). "Not circumcision, nor uncircumcision, but faith which works by love" (Galatians 5:6). In a word, not the professing of Christ but the following of him. *Qui plus habet Christi, plus habet Christianitatis.*[28]

To what purpose is it for a man to be a Protestant if he doesn't cast off the devil as well as his vicar at Rome? To what purpose is it for a man to deny free-will to the good in the unregenerate, if the man remains himself unregenerate? Or, for a man to defend the perseverance of the saints if he be not himself one of the saints? Of what account is it for a man to hold justification by faith and not by good works if the man be himself without faith and good works? What signifies it whether a man be a conformist or a non-conformist if he be still a man conformed to the world? What signifies it whether a man be against infant baptism or for it if the man be not himself washed from the pollutions of wickedness? What signifies it whether a man be for the Presbyterian or Congregational church discipline if he has not a soul under the heavenly discipline? Without the imitation of Christ, all your Christianity is a mere non-entity.

---

[28] "He who has more of Christ has more of Christianity."

Christ's Walk Is an Excellent Walk

Secondly, a Christian should think, "The imitation of the Holy Lord Jesus Christ in my walk will make it become an excellent walk." The more of the Lord Jesus Christ there is in any man the more of excellency there is in that man. Who are the truly excellent? We are informed, "The holy are the excellent" (Psalm 16:3). Now it is in the imitation of Christ that we arrive unto holiness. We then have a holy walk when we walk as he walked. If the question were put, "How shall a man come to be very holy?" The answer would be, "Let a man imitate the example of the Lord Jesus Christ as much as ever he can." It was of old prescribed, "let him that would be an excellent orator set such or such a great master of oratory before him and think just how such a one would manage a cause." Let him that would be an excellent Christian set before himself the example of the Lord Jesus Christ; that will be the ready way to make him one.

The universal imitation of any mere creature may render a man ridiculous. It has been justly decried, "*O Imatatores servum pecus.*"[29] The best man living is not in all things to be imitated. We shall make many blots[30] if, in all things, we write after the copy of the best man alive. Hence the best of men could say, "Be followers of me (only) as I also am of Christ" (1 Corinthians 11:1). It

---

[29] "You imitators, you servile herd..." Mather quoting Horace (*Epistles 1.19.19*).

[30] *Blots* meaning moral stains; disgrace, fault, blemish.

was said, "My Brethren, take the prophets for an example" (James 5:10). But the prophets themselves, all of them had their infirmities. In those very things wherein lay their highest excellencies, they also had their infirmities. Whereas the example of the Lord Jesus Christ is in all things above all exception, the imitation of Christ will never make a man other than excellent. This is the most glittering and massy[31] crown that can be set upon the head of the highest arch-angel in Heaven: to be like unto the Lord Jesus Christ, that Wonderful One, upon whom all the angels of Heaven do employ their eternal praises.

Christ's Condescension
Thirdly, a Christian should think, "Since the Lord Jesus Christ once did look like me, it becomes me now to walk like him." The Lord Jesus Christ hath, in his condescension, made himself like unto us. Shall not we by our imitation labor to be like unto him! We read, "God sent his own Son, in the likeness of sinful flesh" (Romans 8:3). We read, "In all things, it behoved him, to be like unto his brethren" (Hebrews 2:17). Our Lord Jesus Christ would have been God over all, blessed forever, though every one of us were cast away to perish among the firebrands of Hell. Nevertheless, to save us from Hell, our Lord Jesus Christ came from heaven and was made in

---

[31] *Massy* meaning solid and weighty; not hollow, plated, or alloyed.

the likeness of men and was found in fashion as a man.[32] Christian, are you born of a woman? Your Christ said, "Then I will be so too!" So God sent forth his Son made of a woman.[33]

Is there a world of temptation where you are obnoxious[34] in this evil world? Well, your Christ said, "I'll take a taste of it! And so, He was in all points tempted like as we are though without sin.[35] Is your estate wasted? You know your Christ; He became poor[36] for your sake. Is your body pained? Your Christ felt as much when he cried out, "All my bones are out of joint."[37] Is your credit[38] blasted? Your Christ made it his complaint, "Reproach has broken my heart."[39]

Ungrateful man! Shall the Lord Jesus Christ become like you in misery and will not you become like him in sanctification? Argue, therefore, "Oh my Lord Jesus Christ, it was not your honor for You to be made like unto me. It is my greatest honor for me to be like unto You." What shall I render to the Lord Jesus Christ for his coming to feel what I do feel? I will now walk as He did walk!"

---

[32] Philippians 2:7–8.

[33] Galatians 4:4.

[34] *Obnoxious* meaning open to punishment or censure; guilty, blameworthy, reprehensible. *Obsolete.*

[35] Hebrews 4:15.

[36] 2 Corinthians 8:9.

[37] Psalm 22:14.

[38] *Credit* meaning the reputation for truthfulness, accuracy, or honesty.

[39] Psalm 69:20.

Christ, the King of Glory
Fourthly, a Christian should think, "Things less worthy to be followed than the walk of the Lord Jesus Christ, how often are they followed?" Even the unreasonable animals are sometimes imitated by the reasonable. Men count it no shame to imitate the example of the ant and the bee and the birds. What infinite reason then is there that the example of the Lord Jesus Christ be imitated? Children will imitate their fathers. We read of some, "as did their fathers, so do they."[40] Shall not a Christian then imitate him who is the "Everlasting Father" (Isaiah 9:6)?

Subjects will imitate their princes. We read "whatsoever the king did, pleased all the people."[41] Shall not a Christian then imitate him who is "The King of Glory" (Psalm 24:7)? Those persons for whom we have a veneration and an admiration we shall show it by our imitation of them as the friends of Basil did by him. Shall not a Christian then imitate him, whose name is Wonderful? How often have we ourselves imitated even the worst examples and had fellowship with other sinners in their unfruitful works of darkness?[42] Oh, deplorable thing! Sinners are imitated, pagans are imitated, papists[43] are

---

[40] 2 Kings 17:41.
[41] 2 Samuel 3:36.
[42] Ephesians 5:11.
[43] *Papists* meaning Roman Catholics; an advocate of papal supremacy. Chiefly derogatory.

19

imitated, devils are imitated; shall not a glorious Christ be imitated?

We have imitated the first Adam every one of us and we have all sinned after the similitude of Adam's transgression. It is high time for us Christians to imitate the second Adam. The image of the first Adam hath made us forlorn, woeful, doleful[44] creatures. By the image and the imitation of the second Adam, we recover the lost Glory of God.

Walk as Christ on Earth; Walk with Christ in Heaven
Fifthly, a Christian should think, "If I now walk like the Lord Jesus Christ on earth I shall one day be like the Lord Jesus Christ in Heaven." The inexpressible felicity[45] of the future state is best expressed under the notion of a being made like unto the Lord Jesus Christ, or, "To be conformed unto the image of the Son of God" (Romans 8:29). Our Spirits will, in that state, be made very like unto the Spirit of the Lord Jesus Christ for knowledge, for virtue, for unutterable consolations. "Then, we shall be satisfied with his likeness" (Psalm 17:15). Our bodies will, in that state, be made very like unto the body of the Lord Jesus Christ for beauty, for brightness, for spirituality, and for all the endowments of the resurrection. Then "he will change our vile body,

---

[44] *Doleful* meaning fraught with, accompanied by, or causing grief, sorrow, etc.; distressful, gloomy, dreary, dismal.

[45] *Felicity* meaning that which causes or promotes happiness; a source of happiness, a blessing.

that it may be fashioned like unto his glorious body" (Philippians 3:21).

Now it may be enquired, "Who shall be made partakers of this felicity?" There are many marks and signs whereby a person may conclude himself elected, forever to be glorified. But there is none more infallible than this: Christian, do you walk as the Lord Jesus Christ walked? Is it your daily study to be made like the Lord Jesus Christ by an assiduous[46] and industrious imitation of his holy example? If likeness to the Lord Jesus Christ be your sincere study, God will one day give you that likeness to the Lord Jesus Christ for which he shall be admired in you throughout eternal ages. Most emphatic are the words in 1 John 3:2-3, "We know, that when he shall appear, we shall be like him, for we shall see him as he is and every man that hath this hope in him, purifieth himself, even as he is pure."

Walk like the Lord Jesus Christ, Oh Christian, and you shall share with him at the end of the walk. A walker like to the Lord Jesus Christ shall be a joint-heir with him. Our Lord Jesus Christ hath promised concerning those whom he will bless in heavenly places forever: "They shall walk with me." But, who are they that shall walk with the Lord Jesus Christ? Who, but they that now so walk even as he walked.

---

[46] *Assiduous* meaning (of actions): Unremitting, persistent, constant.

The imitation of Christ, do you see a man diligent in this business? I will not now say that man shall stand, and before kings,[47] but I will say that man shall be one of the heavenly kings and the Lord Jesus Christ will grant that man to sit with him on his throne,[48] for the mouth of the Lord himself hath spoken it.[49]

Dwell in Christ Now; Dwell with Christ in Heaven
Sixthly, a Christian should think, "Except I walk like the Lord Jesus Christ in this world, I shall never dwell with the Lord Jesus Christ in the world to come." It was a dreadful commination,[50] "If ye will walk contrary unto me, then will I also walk contrary unto you" (Leviticus 26:23–24). Even so, our Lord Jesus Christ says, "If you do not walk as I walked my terrible and eternal displeasure shall fall upon you." It will be a doom one day falling like a thunder-bolt of death upon the soul of many a man from the mouth of the Lord Jesus Christ, "I never knew you, depart from me" (Matthew 7:23).

Now, who are the men that will not be known to the Lord Jesus Christ? They will be the men that are not like him. We are here a congregation of dying men, but what will become of us when we die? Truly, if we have not walked as the Lord Jesus Christ walked while we

---

[47] Proverbs 22:9.
[48] Revelation 3:21.
[49] Isaiah 58:14.
[50] *Commination* meaning denunciation of punishment or vengeance, especially threatening of Divine punishment or vengeance.

lived, we shall be banished from the Lord Jesus Christ when we die. Because of our crooked ways, we shall be led forth with the workers of iniquity.[51] We are warned, "Many walk, whose end is destruction" (Philippians 3:18-19). Who, but they that walk not as the Lord Jesus Christ walked? Men may hope it shall go well with them in another world and say they hope in the Lord Jesus Christ. But, if they don't walk like the Lord Jesus Christ, their hope is a spider's web which a besom[52] of destruction will sweep down into endless confusion.

Hypocrite, the Lord has rejected your confidences and you shalt not prosper in them.[53] Don't we read, "Christ in you, the hope of glory?" (Colossians 1:27). Truly, if there be anything of Christ in our heart, there will be something of Christ in our walk. Sirs, there is no hope of our coming to glory if we have it not.

Think as such and walk as you think.

III. Meditation as Help for Imitation

By meditation on the holy walk of the Lord Jesus Christ, a Christian will be helped unto the imitation of it and a great elevation of holiness. Contemplation produces imitation. Let a Christian meditate much on those passages of the Holy Scriptures, wherein we have the example of

---

[51] Psalm 28:3.

[52] *Besom* meaning an implement for sweeping, usually made of a bunch of broom, heather, birch, or other twigs bound together round a handle; a broom.

[53] Jeremiah 2:37.

the Lord Jesus Christ exhibited and search the Scriptures which testify of him.[54] It is prescribed as a main direction for our steps in our Christian race, "Looking unto Jesus" (Hebrews 12:2). This thing will produce our walking like to Jesus.

I have read of a great person who had been a most violently and notoriously passionate man, but he afterwards became eminent[55] for his meekness; no man so meek as he! Some wondered at the change and asked him how it came about? He answered, "Oh, it is my much thinking on the meekness of the Lord Jesus Christ that has made me quite another man than what once I was!" Christian, go make the experiment.

Let us not only have our more fixed meditation on the example of the Lord Jesus Christ but also let us have our frequent, our particular, our occasional glances at it. Be able to say with the Psalmist, "I have set the Lord always before me" (Psalm 16:8). There was a king of Bohemia who had a very exemplary father and therefore he always carried his father's picture about him which he would often take out and look on and say, "Let me never do anything unworthy the son of such a father!" Christian, I am sure you have an exemplary Savior and in the Bible you have your Savior's picture before you (It is a popish and sinful folly to have it otherwise, as too many of our people have it hanging on the walls of their

---

[54] John 5:39.
[55] *Eminent* meaning distinguished in character or attainments, or by success in any walk of life.

houses). We will often view it and say, "Let me do nothing that shall be condemned by the example of such a Savior."

When we have any duty to do, think, "How was this duty done by my Lord Jesus Christ?" When we have any trial to bear, think, "How was this trial born by my Lord Jesus Christ?" If we are solicited into any miscarriage,[56] think, "How would my Lord Jesus Christ have entertained such a solicitation? Would the holy and sinless Lamb of God thrown himself into such a puddle of sinfulness?" There are unknown charms of holiness in such meditations.

IV. Supplication as a Help for Imitation

A walk full of supplication to the Lord Jesus Christ is needful for a Christian that would have in his holy walk an imitation of the Lord Jesus Christ. When a Christian takes up secret and serious resolutions to walk as the Lord Jesus Christ walked, let the words of the Lord Jesus Christ come into his mind: "Without me, you can do nothing" (John 15:5). Alas, Christian, you are not able to take one step in the holy walk of the Lord Jesus Christ without strength from him. A man must first become united unto the Lord Jesus Christ by faith and so fetch influences from him before he can be like that holy Lord and walk like him. When we say with ourselves, "I

---

[56] *Miscarriage* meaning an instance of misconduct or misbehavior; a lapse of conduct; a misdemeanor or misdeed. *Obsolete.*

would fain[57] do all things as near as may be like the Lord Jesus Christ," be sure to add, "I can do all things (only) through Christ who strengthens me" (Philippians 4:13). Come then, let us give up ourselves unto the Lord Jesus Christ and choose and make his glory the end of all our walk. But then, let us often repair unto our Lord Jesus Christ, with such prayers as that, "Teach me thy way, O Lord, and I will walk in thy truth" (Psalm 86:11).

V. Suffering as Necessary for Imitation

A Christian must be willing to fare like the Lord Jesus Christ if he will walk like the Lord Jesus Christ. Was not the captain of our salvation made perfect through sufferings? They that will follow that captain cannot avoid many sufferings. Never was there any walk so holy, so watchful, so fruitful, and so blameless as that of our Lord Jesus Christ, who, in his whole walk, went about everywhere doing of good. But could our holy Lord walk so as to have everyone's good word? No. It may be, never man was more spoken against. Simeon foretold it unto his mother concerning him, "Behold He shall be spoken against" (Luke 2:34). Our Lord Jesus Christ had as many enemies as could be. The town and land were full of malignity against him. When he warned the people against the Pharisees, whose horrid covetousness and lasciviousness and impostures he openly detected, they

---

[57] *Fain* meaning gladness, joy.

raised mighty storms of obloquy[58] upon him. When a zeal for the house of his heavenly Father caused him to scourge the thieves out of the temple, do you think they and their sinful friends did not horribly rail at him? Yea, they numbered him with transgressors[59] and laid all sorts of crimes unto his charge. Now, says our Lord, "Remember the word that I said unto you, the servant is not greater than the Lord. If they have persecuted me, they will also persecute you" (John 15:20).

Christians, walk even as the Lord Jesus Christ walked. But now do not fondly expect that everyone should speak well of you. You are no servant of his if they do. It is not so inconsiderable an operation that Satan hath upon a world lying in him that he should not have an army of tongues always ready at his command. There is nothing so vexatious[60] to Satan as the imitation of Christ and therefore the tongues which he can set afire will be sure to spit fire at all that give this provocation. But, Oh Christian, take the great consolation of God! There will no harm come to you by all the harm that any shall speak of you.

It was said, "Who is he that will harm you if you be followers (for so I read it) of him that is good?" (1 Peter 3:13). That is of the Lord Jesus Christ. It is not said, "who will abuse you, who will censure you, who will

---

[58] *Obloquy* meaning verbal abuse directed against a person or thing; detraction, calumny, slander.

[59] Isaiah 53:12; Mark 15:28.

[60] *Vexatious* meaning annoying, irritating.

slander you?" There will be enough and enough to do that. No, but who will harm you? Though they do all of this, there will be no harm to you in any of it.

A renowned person in the English nation, dying on the scaffold, had an abundance of barbarous indignities there heaped upon him at which he uttered this brave speech, "What a deal of pains do they take, to make a sorry sinner like his Blessed Savior?" Truly walk as the Lord Jesus Christ walked and expect vast loads of calumnies.[61] But as they won't stick, so in the midst of them all, think, they are only taking pains to make a sorry sinner like his Blessed Savior.

VI. Courage is Required for Imitation

In fine,[62] a Christian is nothing without courage. That man will never walk as the Lord Jesus Christ walked who is not in his goings like the stately lion which turns not aside for any. This is the full purpose of heart which a Christian is to take up, "I will imitate the holy walk of the Lord Jesus Christ, whatever it cost me."

---

[61] *Calumnies* meaning false and malicious misrepresentations of the words or actions of others, calculated to injure their reputation.

[62] *Fine* meaning a cessation, termination, end, or conclusion of something.

3

THE POINTS IN WHICH A CHRISTIAN SHOULD PURSUE AN IMITATION OF CHRIST

What are the points in which a Christian should pursue an imitation of the Lord Jesus Christ?

The Pythagorean[1] of old had a saying among them, often quoted by many of the pagan ancients, ἕπω θεῷ,[2] "follow God." Some of the ancient Christians explained it and applied it by the call that God gave unto Abraham to follow him.

It is with such a call that you are now to be addressed. Follow God. That is to say, follow the example which that man, who is God as well as man, has given you.

It must not be expected that it will be possible in a few minutes to declare all the points wherein our Lord

---

[1] *Pythagorean* meaning of, relating to, or characteristic of Pythagoras, his followers, or their philosophy. He was born in Samos, Greece. Well-known as a mathematician, scientist, and religious teacher, he was and is often hailed as the first great mathematician.

[2] "The Greek phrase quoted translates literally, 'I follow God,' but Mather elaborates on it as if it had an imperative sense, without reference to the actual person and number of the verb form (ἕπω) he employs."

Jesus Christ is to be proposed as our example. It must be remembered that the virtues of our Lord Jesus Christ are described unto us not only in the Gospels of the New Testament but also in the figures of the Old. The book of Psalms, especially, is a book of the Messiah. You are to apprehend the Lord Jesus Christ a thousand times over, there exhibiting himself as your example, in the language of the Psalmist. Nor are our feeble and foolish essays, when we have done all we can, enough to set off the example of the Lord Jesus Christ in all the fullness and brightness of it. A painter may as well think to paint out the sun in the meridian³ lustre.⁴

But, in the example of our Lord Jesus Christ, we will single out a few more obvious points to be considered.

I. Imitate Christ's Example

The first thing wherein the example of the Lord Jesus Christ gives a lesson to us is the example itself. The lesson we are to learn from the example of our Lord Jesus Christ is that we ought ourselves also to give an example. If the example of the Lord Jesus Christ is to be imitated then his exemplariness is very particularly worthy of our imitation. He that would walk as the Lord Jesus Christ

---

³ *Meridian* meaning of or relating to midday or noon. Often specifically with reference to the position, strength, etc., of the sun at midday.

⁴*Lustre* meaning the quality or condition of shining by reflected light.

walked must walk exemplarily. A Christian must be an exemplary man, exemplary for everything that is holy and just and good. Our Lord Jesus Christ has been an example for us all. In conformity to him, every godly man must endeavor to be an example to other men.

A Christian should be able to bespeak[5] all his neighbors like him in Philippians 3:17: "Brethren, be followers of me, walk so, as you have me for an example." Christians, we must provoke others to good works. How? By setting before them an example of good works and by doing as we have been taught by our Lord, who said, "Let your light so shine before men, that they may see your good works, and glorify your Father which is in heaven" (Matthew 5:16). That is to say, by following of your example. This is a true saying: "*Faelix est illa Anima, que alijs est Forma sanctitatis.*"[6] The greatest glory that can possibly befall any man is to be an example of holiness by which other men may learn to glorify God.

It was a significant reply that John the Baptist gave unto those querists.[7] "They said unto him, 'Who are thou?' And he said, 'I am the voice of one crying in the wilderness about the Messiah'" (John 1:22–23). Do you mind it? He spoke as if he were one all made up of a voice. Even so, if it should be enquired of you, Oh Christian, "Who are you?" it would be well if you were able to

---

[5] *Bespeak* meaning to request or engage (a person) to do (something).

[6] "Blessed is that soul which is a model of holiness to others."

[7] *Querist* meaning a person who asks or enquires.

say, "I am all over a voice. There is a voice in all that I do, bespeaking of acknowledgments unto the Lord Jesus Christ."

It is said of the wicked man, "He speaketh with his feet, he teacheth with his fingers" (Proverbs 6:13). How? Partly by his bad example. On the other side, ought we in our good example to speak with our feet and to teach with our fingers, as I may say.

If Moses could say of all his congregation, "I wish they were all prophets,"[8] give me leave to say for once unto all this congregation, "I wish you may be all preachers!" Every Christian should be in some sort a preacher. It were to be wished that we might every day, all the day long, preach by our example at such a rate that everyone upon the sight of us may say, "Oh! That I might live the life of that man and that my last end may be as his is like to be!"

It is remarked of the great Noah, in Hebrews 11:7, that by preparing the ark he condemned the world. Oh, that our example might so condemn the sensuality and condemn the earthly-mindedness and condemn all the inordinances[9] and irregularities in our neighborhood.

The apostle mentioned it as the singular commendation of the Thessalonians: "Ye became followers of us, and of the Lord, and ye were examples to all that believe, in other places" (1 Thessalonians 1:6–7). May we,

---

[8] Numbers 11:29.

[9] *Inordinances* meaning an inordinate (not regulated, controlled, or restrained) action or practice; an excess.

oh Christians, may we deserve this commendation that we become followers of the Lord and examples unto others how they ought also to follow the Lord.

May we so exemplarily demean ourselves that others beholding our good conversation in Christ may say, "Well, if I would serve God and get safe to heaven, I must walk like such a devout, serious, heavenly man whom I see walking in the narrow way that leads unto a life."

Others' Example Are to Be Imitated

But, if all Christians are to be exemplary, there are some above others from whom all others do look for an example. Those persons that have the charge of other persons are concerned, above others, to be exemplary unto those that they are charged with. Therefore, rulers must be exemplary. When rulers do right or do bad, there is a kind of injunction in their examples; they never do it alone. They should be the first in a good matter and remember that whether they give the word or no, men will follow their leader. It is a sad thing when they that are to restrain and punish vice in others do set a vicious example themselves.

Again, pastors must be exemplary. Those pastors are justly condemned of all men, and the most self-condemned of all men, of whom it cannot be said, "*Hi faciendo docent, qua facienda docent.* "[10] It was urged upon Timothy, "be thou an example to the believers."[11] No atheists are worse than those pretended ministers who say to their poor flocks, "You must do as I say, and not as I do." The Jews have a saying that a crafty wicked man is one of whole things which destroy the world. Now, it is disputed among their Gemarists,[12] "Who is a crafty, wicked man?" And it is answered by some of them, "A crafty wicked man is he who prescribes light things to himself and heavy things to others."[13]

Finally, parents and masters and all superiors in the family must be like so many Abrahams, very exemplary there. Oh! They should not let their inferiors behold the least example of any frowardness[14] or frothiness[15] in them. No, set before them an example of "whatever

---

[10] "These men teach what must be done by doing it," more or less equivalent in sense to the modern phrases "leading by example" or "practicing what one preaches." Mather uses this same quotation elsewhere, in the *Magnalia Christi Americana*. It was probably a favorite saying of his.

[11] 1 Timothy 4:12.

[12] *Gemarist* meaning a student of, or expert on the Gemara, the later of the two portions of the Talmud, consisting of a commentary on the older part (the Mishna).

[13] John Lightfoot, *Matthew-Mark, A Commentary on the New Testament from the Talmud and Hebraica Matthew–I Corinthians* (Grand Rapids: Baker Book House, 1979), 291. Lightfoot's commentary was written in 1658.

[14] *Froward* meaning disposed to go counter to what is demanded or what is reasonable; perverse, difficult to deal with, hard to please.

[15] *Frothiness* meaning having no depth of character, conviction, knowledge, etc.; shallow.

things are lovely."[16] We should be able to bespeak our families as Paul did his Philippians: "Those things that you have seen and heard in me, do, and God shall be with you" (Philippians 4:9).

II. Imitate Christ's Obedience to God

A Christian must endeavor the imitation of Christ in his uniform, universal, and unimitable[17] obedience to the commandments of God. Though we cannot come up to a full imitation of that obedience to God which there was in the whole walk of our Lord Jesus Christ, we must be endeavorous after such a full obedience. When our Lord Jesus Christ was, for us, made under the Law, there was no commandment either of the first or second table in the Law which he did not observe with a most exact obedience unto it. The resolution of our Lord Jesus Christ was "to fulfill all righteousness" (Matthew 3:15); a Christian must resolve like his Lord. The true imitation of Christ is for a man to be continually in that exercise: "I exercise myself to have always a conscience void of offense towards God and towards men" (Acts 24:16).

Avoid Sins of Commission

First, we may be sure sins of commission were altogether avoided in the obedient walk of our Lord Jesus Christ. Our Lord could say to his most critical and censorious

---

[16] Philippians 4:8.
[17] *Unimitable* meaning not deserving of imitation.

and malicious enemies, "Which of you convinceth[18] me of sin?" (John 8:46). Which of them! Oh you spotless Lamb of God, the great God himself, beholding your walk with the flaming eyes of his infinite holiness; he, even he, could never convince you of the least sin against him. Truly we must have been forever condemned for all our sins if our Lord could have been convinced of anyone's sin. He was altogether holy, harmless, undefiled, and separate from sinners when he was made a sacrifice for sinners. He knew no sin when he was made sin.[19] He did no violence to the Law of God in any one instance when God laid on him the iniquities of us all.[20]

Well, we cannot arrive to such a sinless perfection; yet, in imitation of our Lord we should endeavor to walk so that none may convince us of any voluntary, deliberate, indulged sin, and abstain as far as ever we can, even from all appearance of evil.[21] We are charged, "Be blameless and harmless, the sons of God, without rebuke" (Philippians 2:15). Why? By being blameless and harmless we shall imitate the Son of God. Therefore, when we have an invitation to do any ill thing, let the imitation of our Lord be our preservative. Think, "Would my Lord Jesus Christ have done so? No. Nor will his poor disciple."

---

[18] *Convince(th)* meaning to prove or find guilty. *Obsolete.*
[19] 2 Corinthians 5:21.
[20] Isaiah 53:6.
[21] 1 Thessalonians 5:22.

Avoid Sins of Omission

A mere negative religion will never bring a man to positive happiness. We must not only forbear that which is bad but also practice that which is good if we would pretend unto the imitation of our Lord. There were no sins of omission likewise in his obedient walk. Our Lord could say, "I do always those things that please the Father" (John 8:29). Herein must be our study: to do always those things that are like what were done by the Son.

Sirs, do you want an example of love to God? You have that of the Lord Jesus Christ: "I love thee, O Lord my strength."[22] Do you want an example of hope on God? You have that of the Lord Jesus Christ: "Thou art my hope, O Lord God: thou art my trust from my youth."[23] Do you want an example of joy in God? You have that of the Lord Jesus Christ, "The king shall joy in thy strength, O Lord, and in thy salvation how greatly shall he rejoice!"[24] If you would follow the example of the Lord Jesus Christ your thoughts must be full of God and full of heaven. And you must with this often be thinking, "What may I do for the glory of God?" You do not follow the example of the Lord Jesus Christ if your praise be not of God and if you cannot say, "Father, I glorify You!"

---

[22] Psalm 18:1 (David speaking these words to the LORD).
[23] Psalm 71:5.
[24] Psalm 21:1.

Would you follow the example of the Lord Jesus Christ? You must then offer up prayers and supplications with strong crying and tears. Yea, sometimes you must fast as well as pray and spend whole days in cries unto God. And when you have received any favors of God, you must humbly address him with a, "Father, I thank you." He did so!

Would you follow the example of the Lord Jesus Christ? It must be your custom to go into the synagogue where the people of God meet for his worship. You must then hear what God, the Lord, shall speak. You must then take the Book of God to read. You must sing the inspired hymns in the sacred Scriptures. He did so!

Would you follow the example of the Lord Jesus Christ? You must then attend upon the sacraments that God hath appointed. You must receive the baptism of the Lord and the supper of the Lord. You must celebrate the Sabbaths of God. He did so!

Would you not have the example of the Lord Jesus Christ be brought into judgment against you? You must then be subject unto your parents and all your superiors. You must give unto Caesar the things that are Caesar's.[25] You must save the lives of other men and make them comfortable. You must speak well of all that have in them any good things to be spoken of them. You must lay to heart the adversity of your neighbors and be glad at heart for their prosperity. He did all of this!

---

[25] Matthew 22:21.

Except your walk be composed of these Christian duties, you do not walk as the Lord Jesus Christ walked. He could say, "As for me, I walk in my integrity."[26]

III. Imitate Christ's Resistance to Satan

The imitation of Christ must be endeavored by a Christian in resisting the temptations of Satan, who is the great adversary of Christ. One of our grand exercises in this world is to encounter with temptations from that evil spirit whom the Holy Spirit hath called "the prince of this world."[27] That evil spirit, who too successfully fell upon the first Adam with offers of worldly pleasures, riches, and honors to seduce him from his allegiance to God, fell upon the second Adam with the like temptations but not with the like successes. Our Lord Jesus Christ obtained a notable victory over Satan which you find celebrated in the fourth chapters of Matthew and of Luke. Afterwards, by suffering of bruises by that old Serpent, he purchased a share in his victory for all that believe on him; but if we would have a part in the conquest of our Lord over the temptations of Satan we must imitate him in our combat with those temptations.

Reject Satan's Proposals

When Satan does propose unto us any sinful thing, going to charm us with any delights or profits to be gained by

---

[26] Psalm 26:1, 11.
[27] John 12:31; 14:30; John 16:11.

39

that sinful thing, let us reject the proposals of Satan with indignation. Our Lord Jesus Christ did so! He chased away all the tempting devils, with such a word as, "Depart from me, ye evil doers, for I will keep the commandments of my God" (Psalm 119:115). Now since the head overcame this enemy, oh, let not the members yield unto him and his vile solicitations!

Oppose Satan With God's Word

But that we may act with yet more imitation of Christ in resisting and repelling the temptations of Satan, we must oppose them still with what is written in the Word of God. Whatever motion was made by Satan to our Savior, he answered it and defeated it. "It is written! It is written! It is written that the Word of God is, oh Satan, point-blank against every one of thy suggestions."[28] The written Word of God must, in like manner, be awful unto us. We must be able to say with our Lord, "By the word of thy lips, I have kept me from the paths of the Destroyer" (Psalm 17:4). Christian, are you tempted by Satan unto worldliness? Reply, "No Satan, it is written, 'their end is destruction, who mind earthly things.'"[29]

Are you tempted by Satan unto filthiness? Reply, "No, Satan, it is written, 'For the sake of uncleanness, the wrath of God comes on the children of disobedi-

---

[28] Matthew 4:1–10. Jesus' answer to Satan's suggestions, three times, was "It is written."

[29] Philippians 3:19.

ence.'"[30] Are you tempted by Satan unto revengeful-
ness? Reply, "No Satan, it is written, 'Recompense[31] to
no man evil for evil; avenge not yourselves.'"[32] Are you
tempted by Satan unto any dishonesty in your dealings?
Reply, "No, it is written, 'Let no man defraud his brother because the Lord is the avenger of all such.'"[33] Take
this course to confound all the temptations of your subtle adversary; your Savior would have done so! And thus
resisting the devil, he will flee from you as he did from
your Savior.[34]

IV. Imitate Christ's Self-Denial and Humility

Wonderful self-denial and humility and condescension is
one thing wherein a Christian must honor himself by en-
deavoring the imitation of Christ. Pride ruined our first
father. Our great Savior has retrieved that ruin by his
humility. This humility is commended unto us for our
imitation as well as our admiration. Says our self-abasing
Lord, "Learn of me, for I am meek and lowly in heart"
(Matthew 11:29). Therefore, the apostle says, "We
ought not to please ourselves (but laying aside our own

---

[30] Ephesians 5:1–6.
[31] *Recompense* meaning to give in repayment or return; to mete
out in requital.
[32] Romans 12:17, 19.
[33] 1 Thessalonians 4:6.
[34] James 4:7. Mather uses this verse as a commentary on Matthew 4:1–10.

41

humour[35] be ready to accommodate and satisfy one another), for even Christ pleased not himself" (Romans 15:1, 3). Thus, the apostle says, "See that ye abound in this grace (of being ready to part with your own estates for the relief of others), for ye know the grace of our Lord Jesus Christ, that though he was rich, yet for our sakes he became poor" (2 Corinthians 8:7, 9).

Again, the apostle says, "Let nothing be done through vainglory, but in lowliness of mind, let this mind be in you which was also in Christ Jesus, who being in the form of God, thought it not robbery to be equal with God; but made himself of no reputation, humbling himself by taking upon himself the form of a servant, and becoming obedient unto the death of the cross" (Philippians 2:3).[36]

Briefly our Lord Jesus Christ was the heir of all things.[37] Being the Son of God, he had an indisputable claim to infinite and eternal glories. But when the interest and honor of God called for it, he could submit unto the meanest circumstances imaginable. All the angels in heaven owed all possible homage unto our glorious Lord, but our Lord could bear to have his glories eclipsed among the children of men and appear among them un-

---

[35]*Humour* meaning a particular disposition, inclination, or liking, especially one having no apparent ground or reason; a fancy, a whim.

[36] Mather only notes Philippians 2:3, but the entirety of the quote is found in verses 3–8.

[37] Hebrews 1:2.

der such an eclipse that few besides a few poor fishermen should know who he was.

Our Lord was the only begotten and ever-beloved Son of God, and yet he could bear to be treated and sold and scourged like a slave. Our Lord was the maker and builder and owner of heaven itself, but he could bear to sojourn on earth without so much as a house where to lay his head.[38] Our Lord was the rightful judge of the universe, and yet he could bear to be judged among malefactors at the bar[39] of his own creatures. Our Lord had the throne at the right hand of God belonging to him, and yet he could bear to be hanged upon a cross. That face which dazzles the eyes of angels with its lustre could bear to be buffeted and spit upon. That head that had an exceeding and eternal weight of glory,[40] for it could bear to wear a crown of thorns upon it when it was for the interest and honor of God.

Never did humility make such a stoop as in the humiliation of our Lord Jesus Christ! Christian, can you not bear to be little among your neighbors, or to have a veil cast upon your excellencies and does your heart rise and your blood boil and your mind froth and foam at your being overlooked as one of small account in the world? Oh, call to mind the Lord Jesus Christ. He was

---

[38] Matthew 8:20; Luke 9:58.

[39] *Bar* meaning a tribunal, *e.g.* that of reason, public opinion, conscience.

[40] 2 Corinthians 4:17.

infinitely higher than the kings of the earth[41] and yet he could bear to say, "I am a worm and no man, a reproach of men and despised of the people."[42]

Do you count yourself too good to be employed in any good office of Christianity unto your fellow Christian? Your Master Christ did not count himself so when he washed the feet of his disciples and said, "Behold I have given you an example."[43]

Is there any enjoyment and possession too dear for you to part with when God shall call for it? Your Master Christ was willingly stripped of everything at the call and for the sake of God. The Messiah was cut off and had nothing. Oh, look on the humble Jesus and be humbled.

V. Imitate Christ's Zeal Against Sin

Flaming zeal against sin and sinners must be endeavored in the imitation of Christ by a Christian that would not be found a sinner. They that saw the actions of our Lord Jesus Christ could not but remember that portraiture[44] and prophecy once given of him: "The zeal of thy house hath eaten me up" (John 2:17). Such was the holy impatience in the soul of our Lord Jesus Christ when he saw the name of his father trampled upon. Truly, he might

---

[41] Psalm 89:27.

[42] Psalm 22:6.

[43] John 13:5, 15.

[44] *Portraiture* meaning a representation or portrayal through acting, imitation, gesture, etc. Also, a mental image or idea; a type, an exemplar.

say, "I beheld the transgressors and was grieved!"[45] All sin was odious and loathsome to our Lord Jesus Christ. It was part of his description: "Thou hatest wickedness" (Psalm 45:7). Christian, if you can endure and cherish any wickedness, you are not like your holy Lord.

Our Lord Jesus Christ saw some wicked impostors get up to be teachers in the church of God; hypocrites, whose devotions were all to get money and who appeared beautiful outward, but within were full of all uncleanness. How terribly did he thunder out "Woe, Woe," one woe after another against those hypocrites and warn all the people to beware of the serpents! When our Lord Jesus Christ saw abuses creeping into the temple of God what lively castigations[46] did he bestow upon them![47]

When false doctrines were introduced by false teachers with what proper and pungent sermons did our Lord confute[48] them! When his own disciples did sinfully, our Lord Jesus Christ, who loved them so well as to die for them, he would not spare them. No, he would faithfully rebuke his own disciples and the beloved of his soul. His disciples once would have wronged some infants of godly parents by dealing with them as if they

---

[45] Psalm 119:158.

[46] *Castigations* meaning a chastisement, corrective punishment or discipline, correction, chastening.

[47] Matthew 21:12–13.

[48] *Confute* meaning to prove (a person) to be wrong; to convict of error by argument or proof.

were not concerned in the covenant that promises to us the Kingdom of God at the resurrection of the dead.[49] But, we are told in Mark 10:14, "When Jesus saw it, he was much displeased." He did with displeasure let them know that he was very angry at them.

One of his disciples that had very much room in his heart once would only have disheartened him a little in the service of God. But, we are told in Matthew 16:22, "He turned and said unto him, 'Get thee behind me, Satan, thou art an offense to me, for thou favourest not the things that be of God.'" He let him know that there was more of the devil in his offensive speeches than he was aware of.

Christians, bear your testimonies against iniquities and apostasies. Do it with faithfulness and fortitude and let not the wrath of those that make themselves partakers in the sins against which you testify put you out of countenance.[50] Be not afraid of reproving those evil works, which, if you don't reprove, you have a reproveable fellowship with them.

Do what you may, in an orderly way, according to your several capacities for the discountenancing of things that are evidently provoking unto God. Let none of those provocations find you an advocate for them. Let your ardent goodness be displayed in your not bearing with them that are evil, for fear lest the evil that you

---

[49] Mark 10:13.
[50] *Out of countenance* meaning disconcerted or abashed.

could suppress and prevent be made your own. In short, let the precious name of God be as dear to you as your very life. There will be a blessed imitation of Christ in such a zealous inclination.

VI. Imitate Christ's Compassionate Piety

The imitation of Christ must be endeavored by a Christian in a compassionate piety for them whose miseries call for our compassions. The compassion and the tenderness of our Lord Jesus Christ for the miserable is one of the very endearing things by which he hath been signalized unto us. He is a merciful High Priest. He is a High Priest who is touched with the feeling of our infirmities.[51] He is one who hath compassion.

Compassion for Those in Spiritual Misery
Christians, let your hearts bleed with compassion when you see the spiritual miseries of other men. Mourn for the slavery to the powers of darkness wherein you see other men are perishing. Mourn for the perdition[52] in eternal darkness that such multitudes of other men fall into. Mourn for all the blindness and all the hardness and all the sins against God by which you see other men undoing of themselves. There will be an imitation of Christ

---

[51] Hebrews 4:15.

[52] *Perdition* meaning the state of final spiritual ruin or damnation; the consignment of the unredeemed or wicked and impenitent soul to hell; the fate of those in hell; eternal death.

in this compassion. Such was the temper of the Lord Jesus Christ.

When our Lord Jesus Christ saw people starving and pining for want of the means of grace, it cast his bleeding heart into an agony to think, "What shall be done for this poor people?" It is said, "When he saw the multitudes, he was moved with compassion on them. He said to his disciples, 'O pray to the Lord of the Harvest for them'" (Matthew 9:36).[53] And when our Lord Jesus Christ saw persons continue impenitent and unreformed and hard-hearted and unfruitful under the means of grace, it went unto his heart exceedingly. It is said, "He was grieved for the hardness of their hearts" (Mark 3:5).

Compassion for Those in Temporal Misery
Christians, let your hearts melt with compassion when you see the temporal miseries of other men. Be troubled in and for the various troubles with which other men are broken. Visit the sick and comfort the sad and relieve the needy. Help them in all their wants by all the ways you can. Devise liberal[54] things; contrive obliging things when you can do nothing else. Pray for the distressed and stay not until they ask for it, but look out for occasions to do good unto all, especially unto the household of faith.[55] There will be an imitation of Christ in this compassion. It is noted of him, "He healed all that were

---

[53] Mather references 9:36, but paraphrases 9:36–38.
[54] *Liberal* meaning free in giving, generous, magnanimous.
[55] Galatians 6:10.

sick that it might be fulfilled which was spoken by Isaiah the prophet, saying, 'himself took our infirmities, and bare our sicknesses'" (Matthew 8:16–17).

It seems our Lord could not see a sick man but he himself presently felt the sickness of that man and with relenting bowels[56] made it as it were his own! It is said, "Jesus was moved with compassion, and healed their sick" (Matthew 14:14). Hence, when he saw a man that had an impediment in his speech, it is said, "He sighed!" (Mark 7:34).

When he saw people that wanted bread, his charitable heart immediately got so much bread for them as might serve their present necessities. Yea, our Lord never denied anyone that requested a table of his bounty and mercy. But he often did, as for the widow of Naim,[57] with preventing[58] favors, give those to taste of it that made no request unto him. In fine, he that wept over Jerusalem when he saw the miseries hastening upon it, has by the example of his compassion, bespoke[59] our tears for other people that we see becoming miserable.

---

[56] *Bowels* (considered as the seat of the tender and sympathetic emotions, hence): Pity, compassion, feeling, 'heart'. Chiefly *plural*.

[57] Luke 7:11–15. Mather uses Naim, from the Latin Vulgate, rather than Nain.

[58] *Preventing* meaning going before, preceding, anticipating.

[59] *Bespoke* meaning to have borne witness, to have declared to.

VII. Imitate Christ in Profitable Communication

A Christian should endeavor the imitation of Christ in a serious, a savory, a profitable communication with such as come into his company. Of our Lord Jesus Christ, there might always be sung the commendation, "Grace is poured into thy lips" (Psalm 45:2). A gracious discourse was always dropping like honey from the lips of our Lord Jesus Christ. Of them that heard him discourse, it is reported, "They all wondered at the gracious words, which proceeded out of his mouth" (Luke 4:22). Wherever our Lord Jesus Christ came, he constantly let fall some divine, some useful, some noble sentences. No man ever came near unto our Lord but he might hear that which he might go away either the wiser or the better for.

It seems that our Lord was one of a sweet, a kind, an affable[60] conversation; yet, if our Lord were walking on a journey, we find him discoursing on the Scriptures there. If our Lord were sitting at a table, we find him there discoursing on the heavenly feast and the resurrection of the just. And, our Lord would manage his discourses with such a charming ingenuity that he would admirably make all sorts of objects to afford them. He would moralize and spiritualize any sorts of objects and extract notable hints out of anything that occurred unto him and make occasional reflections upon all occurrences.

---

[60] *Affable* meaning easy to approach and converse with.

Now, when you are together, does not the example of the Lord Jesus Christ come upon you as once the Lord himself did upon his disciples with that inquiry, "What manner of communications are these, which ye have one to another?" (Luke 24:17). If you fall into trivial or foolish or mischievous discourse, check them with such a thought as this, "Would my Lord Jesus Christ have talked as I do!" Of him we read, "there was no deceit in his mouth."[61]

Let the imitation of Christ cause you to discourse at such a rate as to do no hurt but some good wherever it is proper for you to discourse at all. You be not like the Lord Jesus Christ if your grammar be not that: "Let no corrupt communication proceed out of your mouth, but that which is good to edify profitably, that it may minister grace to the hearers" (Ephesians 4:29).

VIII. Imitate Christ's Well-Ordered Family

A family well-ordered would be an imitation of Christ, and every Christian that has a family should endeavor it. There is no Christian that has a family but who sees it a thing of great consequence to have a well-ordered family. Christian, are you desirous to know, "How shall my family be ordered?" Order it as the Lord Jesus Christ ordered his. Our Lord Jesus Christ was a master of a family.

---

[61] Isaiah 53:9.

Pray with the Family

First, we find that our Lord prayed with his family. He called his disciples together and then "He lifted up his eyes in prayer before them" (John 17:1). Without doubt, he prayed with them every day that passed over their heads. Yea, and he taught them likewise to pray.

Instruct the Family in the Things of God

But more than this, we also find that our Lord instructed his family in the things of God. It is said, "When he was alone, he expounded all things to his disciples" (Mark 4:34). It was very often that our Lord inculcated[62] upon them the truths of the gospel. And, that his instructions might be the more effectual, he would sometimes call them to an account, "Have you understood my instructions?"[63]

He would also call them aside and examine them concerning their experiences and concerning the state of their souls and the frame of their hearts and what assurances they had attained unto. It was well for the disciples they had cause to bless God forever that they came to live in such a family!

Restrain the Family from Error and Vice

Our Lord was very careful to restrain his family from the errors and vices with which others were carried away.

---

[62] *Inculcated* meaning to have urged on the mind, especially as a principle, an opinion, or a matter of belief.
[63] Matthew 13:51.

He told them what wrong steps were taken by others and he charged them never to tread in the steps. He warned them of the plots that the devil had upon any of them and he showed them how to defeat the plots. There was a time when our Lord foresaw that a multitude of people would go to make him a king. Well that he might preserve all his family from running into the same inconvenience[64] with the rest of the multitude, he beforehand sent them out of the way. Such a watchful eye did our Lord keep up on his family that none of them should be led away with other people into what was not convenient.

Love Your Wife as Christ Loves the Church
I will only add this: it is required of husbands to treat their consorts[65] with all possible goodness and meekness and patience. But, the goodness wherewith our Lord Jesus Christ ever treats his church is to be both the pattern and the motive of their doing so, "Husbands, love your wives, even as Christ also loved the church" (Ephesians 5:25).

IX. Imitate Christ in Your Personal Calling
Christian, you have a personal calling as well as a general. God calls you to an imitation of Christ in the management of it. So follow your calling as to follow your

---

[64] *Inconvenience* meaning moral or ethical unsuitableness; unbecoming or unseemly behavior; impropriety. *Obsolete.*

[65] *Consort* meaning a husband, wife, or spouse.

Savior. Our Lord Jesus Christ had a particular calling. While our Lord led a private life, his calling was that of a carpenter. They said, "Is not this the carpenter?" (Mark 6:3). And, without question, he wrought hard at this calling. I need not bring you quotations from the ancients to ascertain what Basil says, "*Assiduo corporalium laborum exercitio, victum sibi necessarium una cum parentibus pauperibus comparavit.*"[66] But, when our Lord came to lead a public life, his calling was that of a minister. It is expressly said of him, "I say that Jesus Christ was a minister" (Romans 15:8). But how laborious, how sedulous[67] was he in his calling! How faithfully did he fulfill his ministry! He discharged every part of it. He daily did something at the discharge of it; he had no idle time. He often thought with himself, "I must work while it is day. I have but a little time to live. I shall die before I am thirty-three years old. I must lose none of this little time!" And so, he took all advantages to be preaching the gospel of the Kingdom. Every Christian, accordingly, should have a calling.

There should be some special employment by which our usefulness in our neighborhood may be distinguished. We expect benefits from humane society. It is but equal that humane society should receive benefits

---

[66] "Through the constant practice of bodily labors he provided daily sustenance for himself as well as for his impoverished parents."

[67] *Sedulous* meaning to be diligent, active, constant in application to the matter in hand.

from us. Therefore, there should be some special and settled business wherein we that look for the help of other men should be helpful to other men. Well then, let a Christian do the business of his calling like the Lord Jesus Christ, with industry.[68] Be not able ordinarily to take any rest at night if you have not been well at work in the day. Let the example of the Lord powerfully set home that counsel upon you, "Be not slothful in business, but fervent in spirit, serving the Lord" (Romans 12:11).

X. Imitate Christ's Patience

Let patience have its perfect work.[69] Patience is the last and great thing wherein the imitation of Christ is to be the endeavor of a Christian. It is an advice given to Christians, "Ye have need of patience after you have done the will of God."[70] When we have in very many things been doing that which is the will of God in Jesus Christ concerning us, or made known by the example of Jesus Christ as the will of God, still there is one thing more to be learned from the example of our Lord as the perfection of all and that is patience! Patience!

Patient in Affliction

Concerning the Lamb of God, "He was oppressed and he was afflicted, yet he opened not his mouth. He is

---

[68] *Industry* meaning diligence or assiduity in the performance of a task.
[69] James 1:4.
[70] Hebrews 10:36.

brought as a lamb to the slaughter, and as a sheep before her shearers is dumb,[71] so he opened not his mouth" (Isaiah 53:7). Our Lord Jesus Christ underwent sore afflictions from the hand of God. But what was his conduct under all his afflictions? Not the least murmur ever passed from him.

So poor was our Lord that he had not money enough about him to pay his poll-tax. The reputation of our Lord ran so very low that a robber was counted a better man than he. Intolerable pains were inflicted on his body. He lost all his friends; they all forsook him and fled.[72] The powers of darkness were let loose upon him to buffet him with hideous terrors. His eternal Father hid his face from him and seemed wholly deaf to all the cries of the anguish upon him.

What was his behavior under all these direful[73] afflictions! Truly our Lord cast himself down at the foot of the sovereign and righteous God. He had his own will swallowed up in the will of his Father. He bore all the scourges of heaven with a profound submission. Said he, "The cup that my Father hath given me, shall I not drink it!" (John 18:11), and thus, he was dumb, he opened not his mouth.[74] Why? Because You did, Oh Lord, what was done to him.

---

[71]*Dumb* as applied to the lower animals being naturally incapable of articulate speech.

[72] Matthew 26:56.

[73] *Direful* meaning fraught with dire effects; dreadful, terrible.

[74] Isaiah 53:7, which is also quoted in Acts 8:32.

Patient in Persecution

Our Lord Jesus Christ also underwent hard injuries from the hand of man. But what was his conduct under those injuries? He was always doing of kindnesses, even for those that loaded him with injuries. All people fared the better for him. Nevertheless, almost all people belied[75] him, abused him, and maligned him. They accused him of the worst of crimes and laid unto his charge things which he knew not.[76] They never gave over prosecuting their malice against him till they had procured his death. But what resentments had our Lord of these horrid injuries! Truly, none of the indignities done to our Lord could fetch so much as one misbecoming word from his mouth. Hence we read, "Christ hath left us an example, that we should follow his steps, who when he was reviled, reviled not again" (1 Peter 2:21, 23).

Indeed, never did a forgiving spirit so triumph over injuries as in our injured Lord. He could easily have destroyed all his enemies and have revenged himself upon them in their dreadful destruction. Oh! But he forgave them, he pitied them, he prayed for them. Yea, he died for them.

Patient in Crucifixion

I will tell of an astonishing thing. The tormentors of our Lord were gathered like so many fierce devils about him.

---

[75] *Belied* meaning slandered, libeled, calumniated.
[76] "Which he knew not" meaning things he did not do.

They nailed his hands and his feet unto a tree with exquisite barbarity. They lifted up the tree with him hanging in horrible dolour[77] upon it. The falling of the tree with a jerk into the socket prepared for it horribly increased the dolour. Upon this, what was the first cry of our tortured Lord! I do not hear him crying "Oh, my Father, take vengeance on these devils incarnate!" No, but I hear him crying, "Father, forgive them, for they know not what they do." (Luke 23:24). What an astonishing word was this! Forgive them! Who? Ah, Lord, whom would you have to be forgiven! "Father, forgive them that have nailed me to this tree of death."

Final Word

Truly, it is time for me now to break off. I can go no higher. No man did ever attain to such a pitch. Every man should aspire after it.

Christians, if these things are not worthy of imitation, it is impossible to tell the things that are. But, oh, it seems to me the congregation should become a Bochim.[78] We should fall to weeping when we see how little our Lord is imitated in the midst of us.

---

[77] *Dolour* meaning physical suffering, pain. *Obsolete.*

[78] "Bochim is a place name meaning, 'weepers' and is where angel of God announced judgment on Israel at beginning of the period of Judges because they had not destroyed pagan altars but had made covenant treaties with the native inhabitants. Thus the people cried and named the place Bochim (Judges 2:1–5)." Trent C. Butler, "Bochim", in Holman Bible Dictionary. www.studylight.org /dictionaries/hbd/b/bochim.html, 1991. Accessed 11/4/2018.

Analytical Outline

SCRIPTURE INDEX

63

Revelation

Date Completed	Name

H&E Publishing

www.HesedAndEmet.com

About

H&E *Publishing*

H&E Publishing is a Canadian evangelical publishing company located out of Peterborough, Ontario. We exist to provide Christ-exalting, Gospel-centred, and Bible-saturated content aimed to show God to be as glorious and worthy as He truly is.

We seek to provide rich resources that will equip, nourish, and refresh the Christian's soul. We desire to make available a variety of works that serve this purpose in the church. One key area of focus is to revive evangelicals of the past through updated reprints.

ISBN: 978-1-77526-334-0

Fuller deals with the issue of backsliding: when genuine Christians lose their passion for Christ and his kingdom. This was not a theoretical issue for Fuller, therefore, and his words, weighty when he first wrote them, are still worthy of being pondered—and acted upon.

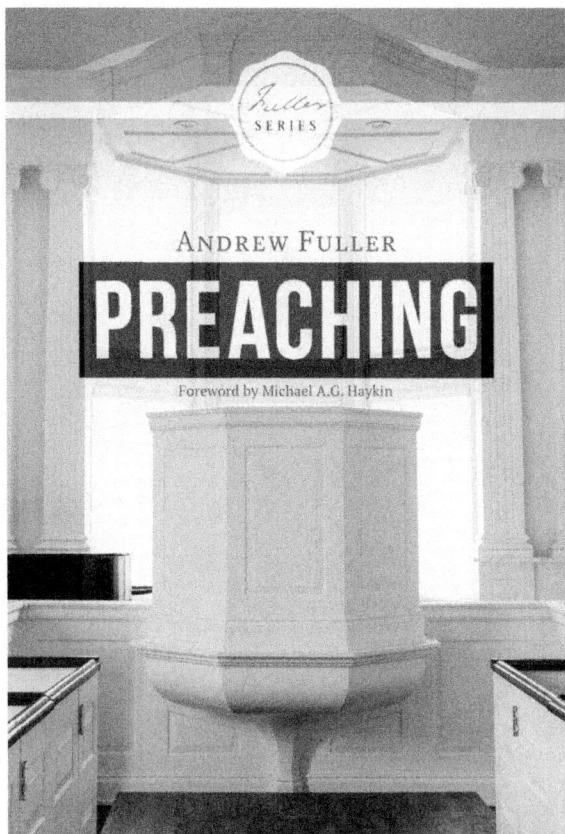

ISBN: 978-1-77526-336-4

Fuller wrote to encourage a young minister in sermon preparation and reading this work will be of great value to any preacher today.

ISBN: 978-1-77526-339-5

In the eyes of Fuller, Samuel Pearce (1766–1799) was the epitome of the spirituality of their community. In fact, in that far-off day of the late eighteenth century Pearce was indeed well known for the anointing that attended his preaching and for the depth of his spirituality. It was said of him that "his ardour ... gave him a kind of ubiquity; as a man and a preacher, he was known, he was felt everywhere."

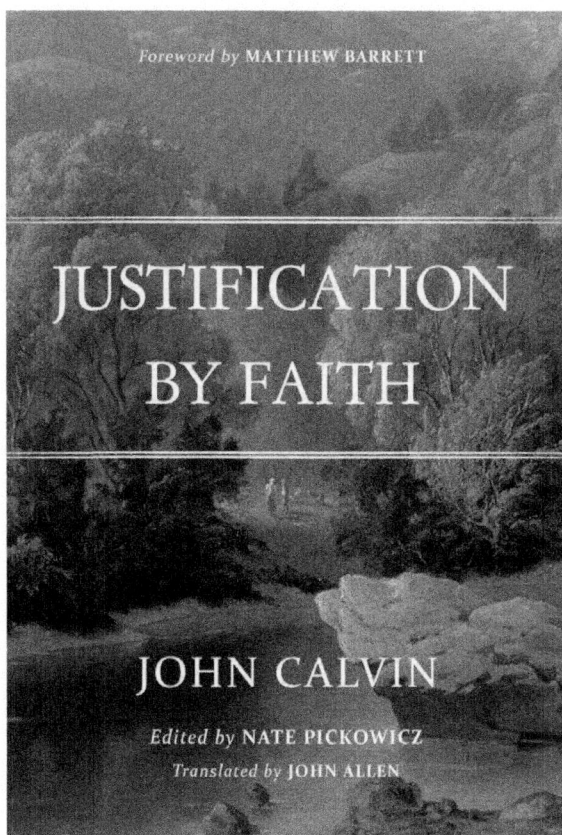

ISBN: 978-1-989174-10-4

Luther was not the only Reformer who spoke about the matter of how a man is Justified, Calvin did too. Here in this work you see the doctrine of Justification by Faith alone thoroughly defended and applied.

MATTHEW HENRY

A CHURCH
IN THE HOUSE

Foreword by Joseph C. Harrod

ISBN: 978-1-7752633-3-3

The famous commentator Matthew Henry addresses the matter of family worship. This classic is useful for any husband and father thinking through the importance of family discipleship.

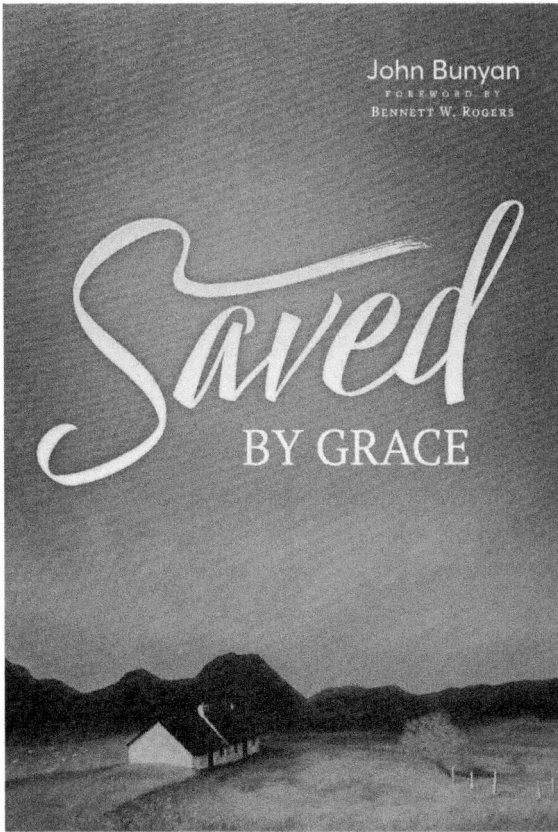

ISBN: 978-1-7752633-2-6

Well known for *The Pilgrms Progress*, John Bunyan writes an extraordinary outline of what it is to not only be saved, but how uniquely it is that we are saved by grace.

Notes:

Notes:

Notes:

<u>Notes:</u>

Notes:

Notes:

Notes:

Printed in Dunstable, United Kingdom

70004493R00058